J 781.7297 ENC

Ench, Rick.

North American Indian
 music /
2x7/03 L 5/03   CHAVEZ-J

S0-CAF-235

North American Indian Music

Rick Ench and Jay Cravath

Franklin Watts
A Division of Scholastic Inc.
New York • Toronto • London • Auckland • Sydney
Mexico City • New Delhi • Hong Kong
Danbury, Connecticut

Note to readers: Definitions for words in **bold** can be found in the Glossary at the back of this book.

Photographs © 2001: AP/Wide World Photos/Kevork Djansezian: 23; Art Resource, NY/Smithsonian American Art Museum, Washington, DC: 7; Corbis-Bettmann: 9 (Nathan Benn), 4 (Philip James Corwin), 32, 36; Jay Cravath: 8 (carved by John Cravath, photo by Peter Crane), 27, 28; Museum of New Mexico, Sante Fe: 29 (neg. #L3316); National Geographic Image Collection/Edward S. Curtis: 45, 47; North Wind Picture Archives: 39 (N. Carter), 11, 25; Sun Valley Video & Photography/nativestock.com/ Marilyn "Angel" Wynn: 3 left, 3 right, 15, 16, 17, 18, 19, 24, 35, 42; The Philbrook Museum of Art, Tulsa, OK: 41; Viesti Collection, Inc./Bruce Montagne: 30, 31; Woodfin Camp & Associates: 12 (Eastcott/Momatiuk).

Cover illustration by Gary Overacre, interpreted from a photograph from © Woodfin Camp & Associates/Suzi Moore.

Library of Congress Cataloging-in-Publication Data

Ench, Rick.
    North American Indian music / by Rick Ench and Jay Cravath
        p. cm. — (Watts library)
    Includes bibliographical references and index.
    Summary: Explores the music of various American Indian cultures, discussing the traditional instruments and the history and meaning of some of their songs.
    ISBN 0-531-11772-3 (lib. bdg.)   0-531-16230-3 (pbk.)
    1. Indians of North America—Music—History and criticism—Juvenile literature. [1. Indians of North America—Music.] I. Cravath, Jay. II. Title. III. Series.

ML3557 .E53 2002
782.62'97—dc21

               2001024891

©2002 Franklin Watts, a Division of Scholastic Inc.
All rights reserved. Published simultaneously in Canada.
Printed in the United States of America.
1 2 3 4 5 6 7 8 9 10 R 11 10 09 08 07 06 05 04 03 02

Contents

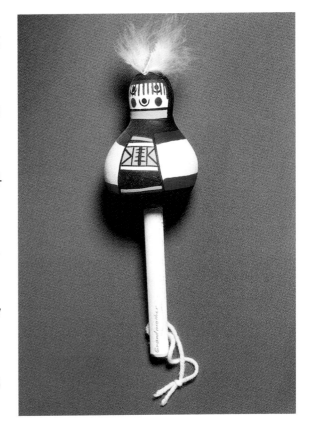

American Indian songs have been sung for thousands of years and continue to live on.

Chapter One

The First Songs

Through the dense woodlands and across the sprawling plains of North America, the sounds of human voices uplifted in song have been heard for thousands of years. The native peoples of America, mistakenly called Indians by early European explorers, have expressed their unique beliefs and ways of life through a wealth of different languages and cultures.

The traditional music of the American Indian tribes has been very important in passing along their beliefs and cultural identity from generation to generation. The traditional songs preserve the **oral history** of each tribe as well as their ceremonies and spiritual traditions. Oral histories are unwritten stories of the past that help define who a people are, where they came from, and how they see their world. An example is the Hopi flute ceremony. The songs ask for a blessing of the crops while retelling stories of the tribe's origins and how they were guided on a great journey that eventually brought them to their present homeland.

To fully appreciate the role music has played in any traditional American Indian culture, it is very important to look at the unique beliefs, ceremonies, and social practices of the specific tribe. Although there are some similarities among the peoples, there are also great differences. This is true even for groups that share similar languages or geographical locations.

Singing With a Purpose

Today, people often write and sing songs to entertain an audience. Many of these songs express emotions or feelings about life and love. Among the traditional American Indian cultures, however, singing to please an audience was unknown. For them, music was far more important than entertainment.

Many of the songs sung by American Indians are similar to prayers. These songs ask for blessings or spiritual help with the tasks and challenges faced by individuals and communities. They are also expressions of gratitude for the things required for survival and success, such as rain to make the crops grow or victory in battle.

The American Indian songs are thought to have great spiritual power. Each song has a specific purpose. For instance, a **healing man**, or woman—also called a medicine man (or woman) or **shaman** by some tribes—can use a song for curing illness. Ceremonial songs celebrate the important stages of life. They are used to mark the coming of age of a young person or mourn the death of a tribal elder.

Songs of origin legends tell how the world was created and how the first people of the tribe came into existence. These songs are like a musical version of the Book of Genesis and other religious texts that describe the beginning of the world. They are usually sung in a series called a song cycle in which one song follows another in very strict order. Almost no tribe that lived north of

This painting shows a medicine man performing a healing ceremony.

Flute Music

The sacred flute ceremony of the **Hopi** of Arizona is still used to court the Corn Maiden **Kachinas** to ensure a successful harvest. In many tribes, flute music was played by a young man to help win the heart of the woman he wished to marry.

Mexico had developed a written language before the arrival of the first Europeans. Teaching these song cycles to the next generation kept the essential belief systems of the tribe alive over the centuries.

The Power of Music

For American Indians, the "Power of Music" is a way of life—an integral part of how the people interact with their world. Although beliefs and religious practices vary from tribe to tribe, these original inhabitants of North America hold some beliefs in common. Among these shared beliefs is the notion that they do not rule over nature. Instead, they think of an animal species as an equal. The **Oglala** Sioux of South Dakota, for example, refer to the bison as the buffalo people.

Everything in their world has a spirit or power that is a small portion of the overall creative power—the Great Spirit of the universe. Songs are used when an individual's power alone is not enough to accomplish whatever needs to be

done. Through song, a man can enhance his own power by calling on the power of other beings in the world to assist him.

For example, an Oglala Sioux healing man may call upon the spirit of a certain herb through song to help him cure a sick child. While the herb is applied to the child's skin in the form of a **poultice** during the process, it is really the spirit of the herb that helps bring about the healing.

The **Iroquois** of the northeastern United States called this universal spirit the **orenda**. They believed that they shared this mysterious power with all created things. Because of this belief, they thought of the animals in their world as brothers

An Iroquois man sings as part of a ceremony in front of a traditional home called a longhouse.

9

and sisters. Songs and the dances that sometimes accompanied them were the primary means of receiving and asserting this spirit power or orenda.

Types of Songs

Among the various American Indian cultures, songs can be placed into four major types. First, there are the ceremonial songs, including the song cycles mentioned earlier. These are believed to have been received in ancient times from the Creator or the guiding spirit beings of the tribe.

Next, there are the songs that individuals receive through a dream or vision. These are often healing songs that assist a medicine man in curing an illness. They can also be songs that young people receive during their **vision quest**. The individual who receives a song in a vision is not considered to be the composer of that song. The song is given to him or her by a spirit who appears in a vision or dream. Nevertheless, once received, the song belongs to this individual.

The third type of song is the composed song. This song is often created by a singer to honor a person who has done something especially brave or to tell the story of an important event.

The fourth type is the **secular** or social song that is used in everyday life for nonreligious purposes. They include lullabies, children's songs, and work songs. Work songs make daily chores seem less tiring. This class also includes songs for sport and games, and songs used to honor acts of courage.

In recent times, through the influence of outside cultures, other kinds of songs have been added to the repertoire of many American Indian peoples. Among these later additions are love songs and traveling songs. Through not traditional in the formal sense, these songs have come to play an important role in the social fabric of many tribes.

A mother sings a lullaby to her child.

These musicians play a large drum, a traditional American Indian instrument.

Chapter Two

Distinct Sounds and Words

American Indian music has a distinct sound in part because it utilizes rhythms and melodies that are unlike those in the music most of us are accustomed to hearing. The cascading melodies of the Plains tribes are a good example. These songs are arranged so that the melody seems to cascade or tumble repeatedly from high to low tones.

Hear It for Yourself

You can play a standard pentatonic scale by using just the black keys on a piano.

Generally, American Indian music has three major components. The first two are beat and **rhythm**. The beat is the underlying pulse of the song, and the rhythm is the sound and silence of the words or music. The third is **melody**. Melody is a progression—or series of tones—that create the tune from a **musical scale** or group of accepted tones, or sounds. Although all music is based on the sensitivities of the human ear, our culture affects the way we hear it. What makes perfect musical sense to the people of one culture may sound strange to those of another culture. As with so many things, beauty is in the eye, or in this case, the ear of the beholder.

In general, most American Indian music is based on a five-note scale. This is called a **pentatonic** scale. The exact notes used in these five-note scales, however, can vary from group to group. The indigenous cultures of North America did not develop a standardized system of **notation** such as the familiar seven-tone Do-Re-Mi-Fa-So-La-Ti scale used in music. As a result, the note progressions of traditional music cannot always be replicated exactly by using a standard pentatonic scale.

Another distinctive quality of American Indian music is its reliance on the human voice as the most prominent feature of the song. The voice usually carries the melody. In addition to the human voice, traditional American Indian cultures uses two categories of instruments to create rhythm and melody. The percussion instruments, which include various types of

The Apache Violin

Although some tribes plucked the string of a hunting bow to make sounds, the **Apache** were the only native people to develop a true stringed instrument. The Apache violin is a one-string instrument that uses a hollowed-out **century plant** stalk as a **resonator**. The Apache may have developed this instrument after they saw the violins of the Mexican people. The true origin of the Apache violin is not known for certain, however, and there is still some controversy about whether or not the Apache developed it independently.

drums and rattles, form the rhythm of the music. Wind instruments, primarily the flute and the whistle, carry the melody in some instances.

Drums

More than five hundred years ago, the most common instrument found in the Americas was the drum. Although there are songs that require only the human voice, such as the prayer cycle songs of the **Navajo**, most of the traditional songs use some form of percussion instrument. More often than not, it is the drum.

The three important classes of drums used in traditional Native American music are hand drums, large group drums, and water drums. The design and construction of each type vary from group to group because of cultural factors and the

A group of singers play hand drums.

natural resources available for making them.

The most common of these drums, the hand drum, is small enough to be held by one singer. Typically, it is constructed with a small hoop made of wood that is covered by a single skin made of animal hide. Some tribes make their hand drums with skins on both the top and the bottom. Hand drums are often decorated with elaborate designs that include symbols and images that have a special meaning for the owner.

The large drum is traditionally made from hollowed logs. This drum rests on the ground and is played by two or more people who sit around it beating the drum in unison, or at the same time. Recently, some drum makers have begun to use metal wash basins and other large round containers instead of hollowed-out logs.

The third class of drum, the water drum, is traditionally made with a log hollowed out on one end only. The other end is left closed to hold water. After native peoples obtained cast iron

Drumsticks

The construction and design of drumsticks also vary from tribe to tribe. The most common drumstick is made of a short narrow stick with a padded knob at one end covered with a piece of rawhide. The Apache use a slender piece of willow bent into a loop at one end for playing their water drums. For many tribes, both the drumsticks and the drums are sacred.

kettles, metal pots, and buckets from the Europeans, they often used these instead of wood. Water drums are usually no more than 18 inches (46 centimeters) in diameter. Animal hide is stretched across the open end and is held in place with a hoop that fits snugly just below the head of the drum. The skin is then dampened with the water from inside and re-tightened. The water in the drum increases its **resonance**, making the drum much louder. A well-constructed water drum can be heard several miles away.

American Indian groups living in areas where wood is scarce, such as the desert, often use other materials to construct their drums. These materials include gourds, woven baskets, and even clay pottery.

Rattles

Most American Indian peoples also use rattles as rhythm instruments. Rattles often accompany drums during a ceremony and are held by dancers who participate in the event. Sometimes they are used instead of drums to provide the rhythm background to a song. The rattle plays an important role in healing rituals. Rhythm patterns are connected to the spirit world, and rattles, like drums, have a sacred significance.

The most common rattle is made from a hollowed-out container filled with pebbles, hard corn,

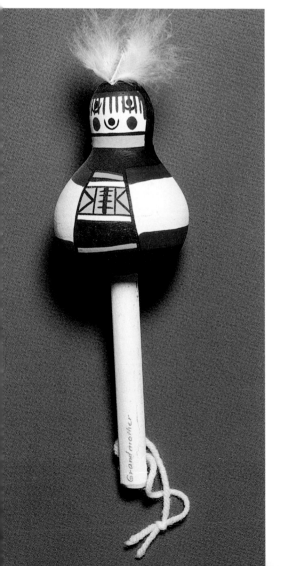

This photograph shows a Hopi rattle made from a gourd.

shells, or other loose objects. The containers are made of wood, gourds, buffalo horns, or turtle shells, and a handle is attached to the container to aid its use. This type of rattle is always shaken by hand.

Other rattles are made by simply hanging small objects, such as pieces of shell or metal, that make sounds against each other. These rattles are often attached to a dancer's lower legs or waist and jingle to the rhythm of the dancers movements.

Finally, another type of rattle may be made from a long piece of wood with a series of notches. This notched wood often rests on a resonator, such as a drum or a gourd cut in half, to increase its volume. A stick is then pulled across the notched wood to produce a rhythmic rattling sound.

A young woman plays a flute, one of the traditional American Indian wind instruments.

Wind Instruments

The term *flute* refers to a class of native wind instruments that are used to play a single melody. A flute has an **embouchure** hole that is blown into like a bottle to make the sound. If the musician doesn't aim the air flow over the embouchure just right, he or she won't get a sound at all. That's why a flute is more difficult to play than a

19

The Bull Roarer

Another noisemaker that employs wind for creating its sound is the bull roarer. This instrument is a short, paddle-like piece of wood that is attached to a cord and whipped through the air in a circular motion by a dancer. It creates a ghostly whirring sound that heightens the atmosphere of mystery in ceremonies.

flageolet, or whistle, where air is blown into a chamber to produce the sound. A common recorder is an example of a flageolet. The tubes for flutes and flageolets are typically 12 to 36 inches (30 to 91 cm) long, and 1 to 2 inches (2.5 to 5 cm) in diameter. Four or more holes are made in the tube. The holes are covered with fingers or are left uncovered to create the different notes. They can be made of a variety of materials including wood, bamboo, or cane. In the Southwest, **Pueblo** tribes, like their ancient cliff-dwelling ancestors, fashion their flutes from clay.

Single-note whistles produce a single note. They are made of various materials, including wood, clay, and bird bones. Whistles are used during ritual ceremonies, including the war dances of many tribes. Since they only produce one note, whistles cannot be used for creating melody, but with their shrill, high-pitched sound they do add to the intensity of the music.

Lyrics of the Songs

In addition to the unique music and instruments, traditional American Indian songs also have distinctive **lyrics**, or words.

Often these lyrics cannot be literally translated into English and still keep their original meaning. Since the people who participate in the ceremony understand the purpose of the song, shortcuts can be taken in the lyrics and many things do not have to be said. The words that are included often highlight the song's meaning but do not always directly state them. Also, there is often a repetition of word sounds that can help bring the listener to the vision that originally inspired the song.

Many of the lyrics of traditional songs cannot be translated because they are not really words at all. These sounds are called **vocables**. They are sounds that have no meaning but are used to carry the melody of the song. A phrase like "Hey-ya-ya-ya, Hey-ya-ya-ya" has no meaning of its own but is still an integral part of the song. These vocables are similar to the meaningless "words" in old rock and roll songs like "be-bop-a-lula." Some vocables may actually be the remains of the tribe's ancient language that are no longer used in conversation.

Among the various tribes, there is a wide difference in how words are used in song. Although many tribes use words sparingly, other tribes have elaborate songs that contain many words. For the song to have its desired effect, these words must be remembered and repeated with flawless precision.

Even when meaning is lost in translation, the beauty and poetry in the words of many traditional songs remain. The following is from the **Sun Dance Ceremony** of the Oglala Sioux:

O **Wakan-Tanka**, I offer You
this world of Light!
This sacred day You made the buffalo roam.
You have made a happy day for the world.
I offer all to You.

Contemporary American Indian Music

Over the last few decades, musicians and songwriters from many North American Indian groups have begun to create new, non-traditional music. This contemporary American Indian music is gaining in popularity among American Indians. Recently, non-Indians have also discovered it. In fact, the year 2001 marked the first year that a separate award category was established for Contemporary American Indian music at the Grammy Awards. The Grammy Awards recognize the best new music in the various categories, including rock, pop, jazz, classical, blues, gospel, and folk during its annual awards ceremony. The first award for contemporary American Indian Music was for the album *Gathering of Nations Pow Wow*.

Contemporary American Indian music composers often use ideas, rhythms, and instruments from traditional American Indian music and combine these with contemporary instruments associated with popular music. These include both acoustic and electric instruments, such as the guitar, bass guitar, modern flute, and keyboards.

Producers Tom Bee (right) and Douglas Spotted Eagle accept the Grammy for Gathering of Nations Pow Wow at the Grammy Awards in Los Angeles on February 21, 2001.

Chapter Three

The Apache Flute Song

The Apache are residents of the Southwest. They live in the forested mountains that are scattered like islands across the deserts of Arizona and New Mexico. The story below is set in the present on the White Mountain Apache reservation in eastern Arizona, the location of famous Fort Apache. In this story, an Apache girl in middle school is awakened by the sound of a flute. It is a boy in her class following the ancient tradition of expressing affection through music.

Culture Day

Brenda Gloshay could hear a flute in her dream. Sweet and flowing, like water, it washed over her. The lonesome sound etched a musical design across her sleep. Birds chirped their way into the dream and followed the song like swallows chasing a raven. That's when she awakened and sat straight up in bed. It was a real flute and they were real birds. It was that Jeff Begay again, playing for her beyond the window.

As she ran to the front porch, she saw that "coyote," flute in hand, racing toward the forest. Flashing a grin at her, he disappeared into the **ponderosa pines** and let out a yell. Brenda yelled with mock anger that she would get him. In playing his flute for her, Jeff was following an ages-old tradition. An Apache boy attracted to a girl would play a song outside her home to make her heart feel lonely and seek its cause.

The Begay family follows the traditional practices of the Apache, such as singing and winter storytelling. Winter was used for storytelling because this was when the animals were asleep, and would not be offended to hear tales and songs about themselves, some of which might not be so flattering. But this was May and the White

Opposite: An Apache woman walks in a field on the White Mountain Apache reservation.

Young men have been playing their flutes for young women for hundreds of years.

25

Mountains were alive with flowers. Flutes were fine for playing. They called plants out of the earth and brought rain clouds for the corn and squash in the garden. They also helped girls fall in love.

Brenda smiled and shook her head. She liked that Jeff Begay. She'd have a surprise for him when she sang at the school's Culture Day assembly that afternoon.

On their way to the bus stop that morning, her younger brother Timothy carried the water drum Brenda used to accompany her social songs. The drum was actually an aluminium cooking pot without a handle. Cowhide was stretched over the top and held in place by a thin strip of rubber tire tubing. Timothy sloshed the water inside, soaking the top. He began beating the drum skin and singing a goat song:

> Hey ney ya-a hey, hey ney ya-a hey,
> hey ya hey ya hey ya.
> Clizi sana hi nie lostong-o
> toho t'ush ong- o-o Hey ney ya.

They arrived at the bus stop just as the song finished. Their old bus rattled to a stop, and soon they were on their way into school.

At the Culture Day assembly that afternoon, the students of East Fork Middle School were packed into the auditorium. When Brenda announced her last song to the crowd, the "Apache Love Call," she dedicated it to Jeff Begay who was

behind the stage preparing to perform the Apache War Dance. The crowd made an "ooooing" sound. Brenda smiled and began to sing:

This photograph shows a young woman performing the Apache Love Call song.

> Ey ney yo ha ey ney yo ha
> Ey ney yo ha- ya na ha ya na ha hi ya
> Aya be-ets o see tazhi ay bigala tazhi
> Ha see ya agan seego she na sha hi ya

When Brenda was finished, the audience applauded, giving a few shouts here and there. Then the curtain opened, and Jeff and his partner faced each other in traditional Apache war costumes, each holding a spear and shield. Their dance was very exciting and received hearty applause.

Apache Love Call

Helen Crocker, a White Mountain Apache elder, provided this song for the book. It begins in a slow two-beat tempo and speeds up when it comes to "Aya be-ets o see tazhi," where it moves to a fast dance beat. Changes in tempo are common in Apache music.

These Apache are participating in the "Back and Forth" dance.

All the performers came on stage for the closing social dance called the "**Back and Forth**." They formed a line at the front of the stage with arms interlocked. When the song started, Brenda felt someone take her arm. She looked over to see Jeff, who had chosen to dance with her in front of the

whole student body. Her face flushed, but she matched his steps as the line moved four steps forward and four steps back. That Begay—he'd gotten the last laugh!

Natalie Curtis: Song Maid

The Hopi called her Tawi-Mana, the Song Maid. She set an ambitious mission for herself in the early 1900s—to record the music and stories of as many American Indian tribes as possible. To accomplish this, she carried her bulky wax cylinder (an early form of phonograph) across the United States to preserve Indian music for future generations. From the **Wabanaki** of Maine to the **Kwakiutl** of the Pacific Northwest, Curtis recorded and transcribed songs and stories from many tribes. She was known as an **ethnomusicologist**, a person who studies music of a cultural or ethnic group.

There are more than 100,000 Ojibwa Indians living in the United States today. They are also known as the Chippewa.

Chapter Four

The Ojibwa Medicine Song

The Ojibwa are a northern woodlands people. Their traditional homeland is the forests of the Great Lakes region of Wisconsin, Minnesota, Michigan, and southern Canada. They hunted game and fish and lived in **wigwams**—houses made from poles tied together to form a dome and covered with bark or skins. The following story is about a boy who has been called by the Great Spirit to become a shaman. Despite his youth, his special power is widely respected.

The Gift of Healing

The snow crunched underneath as Margaret Wampum Hair and her husband George walked the peninsula following a boy of about fourteen. He had a long fishing pole over his shoulder and stood at a point where lake water was lapping snow off the grey rocks. The day was sunny but bitterly cold as they reached the boy. His name was Pierre La Blanc. He belonged to a healing society known as the **Midewiwin**, a secret organization that kept the ancient medicine of the Ojibwa alive. Pierre had been receiving messages through his dreams since he was very young. He lived in a wigwam he had built next to

This photograph shows a traditional Ojibwa wigwam.

his parents' house. His uncle often came by for him in the mornings. They fasted together. Uncle Jack taught the boy many medicine songs and helped him construct a special healing drum. It resembled a tambourine without the metal rings but had pebbles inside that rattled. The skins were painted red and black.

Pierre knew what they wanted and told them his time for medicine had not yet come. But Mrs. Wampum Hair insisted that she was certain he could help. The boy reluctantly agreed and said he would come to their house.

The Wampum Hairs returned to their daughter. She was on a couch in their small living room, covered with a red and white woolen blanket. A wood stove crackled with dry pine, sending warmth and fragrance into the room.

A little later, they heard the boy outside singing a blessing for the house. When he was done, Mr. Wampum Hair opened the front door. The boy motioned for him to help place a pole in the ground with a rattle at the top. Then they went back inside. The boy took out his drum and sat on the floor next to the girl. He began to beat softly with an L-shaped stick, singing:

| Kezhegukin | When it is day |
| wayashkun ah kee | the earth is illuminated |

The boy repeated the phrase three more times while Mrs. Wampum Hair sat nearby with her eyes closed. The boy lit a

Teaching Songs

On the path to becoming a medicine person, it is essential to have a teacher. For songs to have power, they must be sung perfectly.

A Sculpture to Help the Maple Sap Flow

The Ojibwa people traditionally gather maple sugar in the early spring. If the weather got too warm, the tree sap would not run into the buckets hanging on the trees but would instead be absorbed into the wood. To counteract this, the medicine man might make a rabbit sculpture in the snow. It faced north and was given a silly expression on its face to tease the north wind during maple sugar gathering. The north wind would see the rabbit mocking him and try to blow it down. The harder it blew, the stiffer the rabbit would become, and so the sap would run smoothly.

clay pipe filled with **kinnikinnick**, a dried plant that was smoked ceremonially. As the boy smoked next to the girl, the rattle on the pole began to shake even though there was no wind. The boy finished and said he would return later.

At dusk the boy returned, carrying his drum. He put some dried flowers in a dish and poured hot water over them from an old copper kettle on the wood stove. The water turned a bluish color. The boy reached down to a leather pouch on his belt and took out seven small bird bones. He placed them in the dish with the flower water. Then the boy took them from the dish and placed them in his mouth. He removed the bones one by one and placed them on a white cloth covering the girl's chest. The boy got his drum and sat on the floor in front of the girl. He sang four songs and then stood up. Mr. Wampum Hair saw him to the door.

The next day the boy came back to the house. Mrs. Wampum Hair opened the door and smiled, saying the girl was much better. Mr. Wampum Hair called him

Kinnikinnick was used as part of the healing ceremony.

"Kihci-na'pe'," an important man, and gave him a frozen **sturgeon**. The boy nodded and walked away on a trail that led into the forest.

Sitting Bull was one of the leaders of the Oglala Sioux.

Chapter Five

Oglala Sioux Vision Quest

The Oglala Sioux are a people of the northern Great Plains who lived by hunting the buffalo. They were known as great warriors, and their chiefs included **Crazy Horse** and **Sitting Bull**. The larger Siouan nation has traditionally ranged from Lake Michigan to the Rocky Mountains. The word *Sioux* is an insult originating from their Algonquin neighbors, and it means "snake" or "enemy."

The following story tells of a young boy who undertakes the Oglala Sioux coming-of-age ceremony known as the vision quest. Selected men of the tribe will help this boy to manhood by instructing him in finding his own vision for the future and his special song.

The Vision—Part One

Alex Little Crow was about to begin the most important journey of his twelve years—a vision quest. His hope was to find his animal guide and his special song. Alex listened as Spotted Hawk recounted the story of Ptesan Win, White Buffalo Woman. Long ago, Wakan-Tanka, the Creator, sent her to the Oglala Sioux people to teach them how to use the sacred smoking pipe, as well as how to pray and sing the songs. This was when woolly mammoths still walked the earth. The Oglala Sioux language was crude then, and people did not know how to pray.

White Buffalo Woman

White Buffalo Woman first appeared to two hunters. She told them to return to their village and tell everyone to get ready to receive her. They had to prepare a sacred teepee and a sweat lodge. When White Buffalo Woman entered the village, her voice was sweet and she was very beautiful. She carried a sacred rock with seven carved circles for the seven sacred rituals of the **Lakota** Sioux nation. White Buffalo Woman instructed the people in the sacred ceremonies. She showed the women how to do **quillwork**, and she taught the men to hunt and to protect the women and children. After the people learned the holy knowledge of Wakan-Tanka, White Buffalo Woman disappeared into the clouds.

Sweat Lodges

The sweat lodge is like a sauna or steam bath. Rocks, heated in a fire, are placed inside a small enclosure, and water is poured over the rocks to make steam. Many tribes use sweat lodges as a purification ritual before sacred ceremonies.

At sunrise, Spotted Hawk sang the song of White Buffalo Woman when she appeared to the ancestors:

Niya taninyan	With visible breath
mawinaye	I am talking.
oyate le	Toward this nation
imawani	I am walking.

The song of White Buffalo Woman stuck in Alex's head as the sweat lodge was prepared. It calmed his racing heart.

Spotted Hawk lifted the canvas door of the sweat lodge and motioned for Alex to enter. The lodge had a dome shape and was made of sixteen willow branches covered with canvas cloth. As Alex sat cross-legged inside, he could smell the sage scattered on the floor. Sage is a holy herb that welcomes the spirits. A circle with seven heated stones was in the middle of the lodge. The stones represented the four directions as well as above, below, and here. Alex's uncle, Tiny Man, brought in a bucket of water and poured it over the stones. Steam hissed through the dark space as the two men sat down next to Alex.

Spotted Hawk began singing the songs. Alex could see a faint orange glow from the stones. The heat from the steam seemed unbearable but he remained silent. He prayed to Wakan-Tanka, the Holy Grandfather (the Creator), for courage. Spirits whispered to him in spirit language. The sweat ended with the smoking of willow bark tobacco in a sacred pipe. Spotted Hawk asked for Wakan-Tanka's blessing on the boy in his vision quest.

Alex, Spotted Hawk, and Tiny Man left the sweat lodge, following a trail that snaked up through a stand of juniper. Alex was told to remove his shoes so he would be in touch with sacred Earth. When they reached the vision pit, Spotted Hawk told Alex to walk around it four times. The pit was dug about 4 feet (1 meter) into the ground and was covered with brush. Alex was to spend the next four days inside it without food or water, waiting for his vision. Spotted Hawk instructed him to think good thoughts, and to bring back messages for himself and his people.

The men left and Alex was alone. Fear gripped him, but he prayed and waited. Day turned to night. He heard an owl,

Animal Guides

The Sioux believe that an animal who appears during a vision quest becomes a special guide throughout the individual's life. For example, a red-tailed hawk seen during the vision is said to reappear at crucial moments in that person's life to assist with important decisions.

This painting depicts a spiritual vision.

crickets, and a coyote howling in the distance. The next day Alex drifted in and out of sleep, trying not to think about food or water.

By the third day he no longer felt hunger or thirst. It was at this point that his vision began. Rainbow colors ran past his eyes, and white lights flickered in the brush roof above his head. Suddenly, he saw the face of a deer. It spoke to him, telling the story of his people, of their suffering and hardships. It taught him ways to help the people. Then it taught him a song: "Wakan micage (Sacred he made for me) Wakan micage, Sinte sapela wan (a Blacktail deer)." A gopher appeared and danced to the song as colors continued to swirl around them.

Alex felt the arms of someone lift him from his dream and gently pull him out of the pit into the afternoon sunlight. He was carried down the trail to the sweat lodge to reveal his vision, and was then set on a blanket next to the lodge. Before he could talk or enter the sweat lodge, he was told to eat the prepared food, spoonfuls of corn and water. Alex felt happy and proud. He was ready to tell his vision and sing his song.

This photograph shows one of the performers at a Kwakiutl ceremony.

Chapter Six

The Kwakiutl Winter Ceremonial

The Kwakiutl of British Columbia, Canada, are one of the many tribes who inhabit the Pacific Northwest coastal region stretching from Oregon to southeastern Alaska. They were traditionally known for their huge seagoing dugout canoes, large **cedar plank** houses, and elaborate wood carvings. Their name, *Kwakiutl*, means "smoke-of-the-world,"

Warrior-of-the-World

One of the most important of the Kwakiutl **deities** was Warrior-of-the-World. He was taller than any human and very slim. He had a black body and bat-like eyes. Never leaving his canoe, he traveled constantly. Some wear masks of this deity during ceremonies.

a reference to the smoke rising from the many fires of those who attended their elaborate ceremonies called **potlaches**. These are feasts during which powerful and wealthy hosts give away blankets and many other items, thereby proving their generosity and securing their high social position. Though not as elaborate as in the past, potlaches are still held today.

The following story is based on a description of the 1902 Winter Ceremonial, which lasted from November to March. It was a series of complex religious and theatrical performances that included much singing and dance. The ceremonial honored the supernatural beings who, the Kwakiutl believed, came to reside in their villages after spending the summer in distant lands. It took place during feasts in large village meetinghouses.

Salmon-Girl's Initiation

Salmon-Girl sat in a small dark room with two women by her side. She had been invited by her uncle, Wind-off-Sea, to her first ceremonial. Since she was coming of age, he would be host to her initiation into the young women's society, q!o'minaga—the Birds. She now waited in a small room behind the meetinghouse where the people of the village sat in rows on colored blankets. It was night, and small fires in the feast room flickered like dancing lights while their smoke wafted up through holes in the thatched roof. Wind-off-Sea gave a speech thanking all the people for coming and asked the audience to have their batons ready. These sticks would be used to hit the long cedar planks that served as communal drums during the songs.

Before Salmon-Girl was allowed to enter, from the small waiting room, the seated people were fed a meal of crabapples mixed with grease. Then the **Cormorants** arrived. These two men, dressed as sea birds, flapped their arms and then took

Cedar Plank Drums

During potlaches and the Winter Ceremonial, long planks of cedar wood were brought to the feasts for people to hit with batons during the songs.

These two dancers are dressed as mythical birds.

their places at one end of the room. The host thanked them for coming from the far corners of the world. A song began, which was the signal for the **Orcas**, the killer whales, to enter by twos and threes. Their fins of wood stood up straight as they shuffled in bent over, making blowing sounds. They "swam" to the Cormorants and stood up. Then women dressed as various birds entered.

Salmon-Girl heard the song made by her mother for this occasion. It was the signal for her entrance:

> This is my gift who digs clams for her mother,
> > ahey ahey ya
> This is my gift who digs roots for her mother,
> > ahey ahey ya

Salmon-Girl entered the room with her two attendants. She was dressed in a blanket and dancing apron, and she wore a **neckring**. On her head was a ring covered with down. As she appeared, the women of the Bird society began to dance. The girl took her place at the main fire in the middle and danced to the music. During the next song, which was traditional, the seated people beat on the cedar planks with their batons and sang along.

After the song, the girl sat next to the fire. Then, a man was heard at the front door singing a sacred song. The door opened and he entered, wearing only an apron with a cedar bark headring and anklets. He held a magical throwing stick.

The Thrower of Sickness wore a cedar headring and carried a staff similar to the man in this photograph.

47

Kwakiutl Societies

Membership in these groups was passed down through a family. Each Society performed important ritual roles in the tribe's ceremonials.

The Thrower of Sickness had arrived, and the seated people recoiled in fear. A hand drum beat wildly as he acted out an illness. He rolled on the floor in unusual contortions, spitting out the animal blood he held in his mouth. Salmon-Girl watched in awe. Suddenly he was still. Shamans were called to sing over him. After the fourth song, the Thrower of Sickness stood up, now healed. This healing signaled the end of the ceremony.

Salmon-Girl felt happy. She looked forward to learning all the songs for the Winter Ceremonial, and she planned to make a song of thanks to her uncle for this wonderful initiation.

Glossary

Apache—an Athapascan language-speaking people whose traditional homeland includes parts of Arizona, New Mexico, Texas, and Northern Mexico

Back and Forth—a social dance of the Apache where partners link elbows and dance four steps forward and four steps backward, repeating the sequence through the song

cedar plank—a plank from a felled Cedar tree that could be used for houses or carried into ceremonies to be used as communal drums

century plant—a plant that blossoms only once every ten to twenty years and then dies

cormorant—a dark-colored, web-footed sea bird of the family *Phalacrocoracidae*. It has a long neck, hooked bill, and wedge-shaped tail.

Crazy Horse—an Oglala Sioux war chief who led a group of

Sioux and Cheyenne against Colonel George Armstrong Custer in the Battle of the Little Big Horn

deity—a god or goddess

embouchure—the mouthpiece of a wind instrument. The embouchure has a notch (end-blown flutes) or a hole (transverse flutes) where air is blown across to create sound vibrations that become musical tones.

ethnomusicologist—a social scientist who specializes in the study of music in a cultural or ethnic context

flageolet—a flute-like wind instrument with a tube-like mouthpiece that air is blown into. The sound vibrations are created within a small chamber in the mouthpiece. Finger holes are then covered or left uncovered to create a range of musical tones.

healing man (or woman)—a specialist in traditional Native American medicine

Hopi—a Pueblo people whose traditional villages of stone and adobe sit atop the mesas of northeastern Arizona. They are believed to be the descendants of the cliff-dwelling peoples that once occupied many areas in the Southwest.

Iroquois—a confederacy of northeastern woodlands peoples who spoke related languages and whose traditional homeland includes upstate New York and parts of Pennsylvania and southern Canada. The Iroquois Confederacy now includes the Cayuga, Mohawk, Seneca, Oneida, Onondaga, and Tuscarora tribes.

Kachina—one of the ancestral spirit beings of the Hopi people of the Southwest. They are believed by the Hopi to bring the rain and assist them in other ways. Dolls based on the Kachina costumes worn during Hopi ceremonials are carved and decorated by Hopi artists and sold to the public.

kinnikinick—a mixture of dried leaves, bark, and sometimes tobacco that was smoked during some native ceremonies

Kwakiutl—an American Indian tribe whose traditional home is along coastal Washington and British Columbia. The word translates as "smoke of the world" in their native language.

Lakota—one of the seven main groups of the Sioux

lyrics—the words and vocables that are sung by the singer of a song

melody—a sequence of single musical notes related to one another in such a way that they create a recognizable tune

Midewiwin—an Ojibwa medicine society whose members display a unique relationship with the spirits. Much of their healing is done with the use of song.

musical scale—an ascending or descending series of musical tones that have a predetermined scheme of intervals between one tone and the next.

Navajo—an Athapascan-speaking American Indian tribe occupying a large reservation located in Arizona, New Mexico, and Utah

neckring—a type of Kwakiutl ornamental necklace often decorated with feathers

notation—a system of figures or symbols used in music to represent specific tones and combinations of tones.

Oglala—One of the Siouan language-speaking groups of Native Americans whose traditional home is the northern great plains including the Dakotas, Nebraska, and Montana

oral history—unwritten accounts of past events used by cultures that have not developed written language

orca—a large carnivorous member of the whale family commonly known as the killer whales

orenda—a sacred force or power believed by the Iroquois to be possessed by all things. This power could be used by a holy man to cure illness or accomplish miraculous feats.

pentatonic scale—any of the various five-note musical scales; the most common being the first, second, third, fifth, and sixth tones of the standard diatonic, seven-note scale

ponderosa pine—an evergreen conifer with the species name of *Pinus ponderosa* that grows throughout western North America

potlach—an elaborate feast of the Kwakiutl and other Northwest coast tribes during which many items are given away to demonstrate the hosts' personal wealth and generosity

poultice—a warm, moist mass of soft clay, meal or plants that is spread on an area of the body to bring about healing and relief from pain

Pueblo—various tribal groups in the southwestern United States whose traditional villages are comprised of multi-storied community dwellings made of adobe or stone. Both the dwellings and the village itself are referred to as pueblos. *Pueblo* is the Spanish word for "town."

quillwork—an Indian handicraft where porcupine quills are interwoven to decorate various kinds of clothing

resonance—the intensifying and prolonging of musical tones produced by sympathetic vibrations within a resonator

resonator—a hollow chamber or cavity with a size and shape that permits sound waves to vibrate within it, substantially increasing their volume or loudness

rhythm—a regular pattern of sound and silence formed by a series of musical notes of differing duration and stress

secular—not related to a religious practice or ceremony

shaman—a word used for a medicine man or medicine woman among some North American Indian groups

Sitting Bull—a famous medicine man and leader of the Hunkpapa Sioux. He helped defeat George Armstrong Custer in the Battle of the Little Big Horn and later fled to Canada.

sturgeon—a large edible fish of the genus *Acipenser*. The roe, or egg sack, is used for caviar.

Sun Dance Ceremony—a traditional ceremony of the Sioux peoples of the Great Plains. The ceremony, which can produce visionary states, is used to bring the blessings of spiritual assistance to the participant and his community.

vision quest—a ritual practiced by many American Indian groups that often served to mark a boy's coming-of-age. Usually, after a purification ritual, a boy of 12 or 13 stays at a remote location alone, remaining awake and fasting until he receives a dreamlike vision that will assist him with his future life.

vocable—a meaningless word sound that are used to forward the melody and rhythm of a song

Wabanaki—a group of American Indians in Maine known for their beautifully beaded Wampum belts

Wakan-Tanka—the Sioux reference to the "Great Spirit" or God

wigwam—a traditional dwelling of many northeastern tribes of the United States, it had slender poles in a circle placed in the ground and tied together at the top. Sheets of birch bark covered the structure for waterproofing, and bark and grass were tied in bundles for insulation.

To Find Out More

Books

Ball, Jeff. *Trailhead of the American Indian Courting Flute.* Lafayette, CO: Four Winds Trading Co., 1994.

Burton, Bryan. *Moving Within the Circle: Contemporary Native American Music and Dance.* Danbury, CT: World Music Press, 1995.

Curtis, Natalie. *The Indians' Book.* Mineola, NY: Dover Publications, 1968.

Fletcher, Alice C. *Indian Games and Dances with Native Songs: Arranged from American Indian Ceremonials and Sports.* Lincoln, NE: University of Nebraska Press, 1994.

Greene, Jacqueline D. *Powwow, A Good Day to Dance*. Danbury, CT: Franklin Watts, 1998.

Swann, Brian, ed. *Native American Songs and Poems*. Mineola, NY: Dover Publications, 1997.

Organizations and Online Sites

The National Museum of the American Indian
One Bowling Green
New York, NY 10004
http://www.nmai.si.org/
Part of the Smithsonian Institution, this museum offers exhibits and educational programs on the native peoples of the Americas.

Native American Music Awards
http://www.nativeamericanmusic.com
This online site provides information about past award winners, and visitors can listen to Native American music through its online radio station.

Ohwejagehka: Ha `degaenage
http://www.ohwejagehka.com
This Ontario, Canada-based organization is devoted to preserving the language and songs of the Iroquois. From its online site, visitors can learn more about the Iroquoian songs.

White Mountain Apache

http://www.wmat.nsn.edu

Learn more about the White Mountain Apache from their official online site.

A Note on Sources

Sources for the first three chapters of the book that focus on the general nature of American Indian music includes Frances Densmore's carefully researched book on the subject, *American Indian Music*. It was written over seventy years ago, at a time when tribes practiced many more ceremonies than they do today. M. Herndon's book, *Native American Music*, was helpful because it not only compares various ceremonies, but also lists ethnomusicologists and their work with specific tribes. *The Indians' Book* by Natalie Curtis is also an excellent source for comparing Native music. It is filled with transcribed songs (that means written down with lyrics and notation) and stories of the musicians she met when recording and studying various groups.

The tribes chosen for this book have been studied extensively by ethnomusicologists. Frances Densmore's *Teton Sioux Music*, which has music and descriptions from many rituals, was helpful as was *Crow Dog* by R. Erdoes, about the life and work of a Sioux medicine man. For the Kwakiutl, the work of Franz Boas is unmatched and can be found in *Kwakiutl Ethnography*. It is an excellent book that combines many of his writings and includes songs and extensive descriptions of their use in ceremonies. For the White Mountain Apache, J. Haley's *Apaches: A History and Culture Portrait* was an excellent source. Also, *The People Called Apache* by T. S. Mails combines the author's beautiful illustrations with lots of information.

The musical and spiritual practices of the Ojibwa are outlined at length in the R. Landes book, *Ojibwa Religion*. Our source for information on growing up in the traditional Ojibwa culture included *Portage Lake: Memories of an Ojibwa Childhood* by M. Kegg, and *Ojibwa Narratives* by C. Kawbawgam.

Finally, the authors of this book, having been involved with American Indian music and ceremony for the last twenty years, used a number of personal sources to illuminate the text.

—Rick Ench and Jay Cravath

Index

Numbers in *italics* indicate illustrations.

About the Authors

Rick Ench is a writer and filmmaker who has written and directed several documentaries on American Indian subjects, including the series *The History of the Western Apache*, and the films, *Love Is a Child* and *A Thousand Years of Song*.

Jay Cravath is an educator, composer, and performer. He received the NEH-Reader's Digest Teacher-Scholar grant to do full-time research in ethnomusicology and also the Arizona Humanities Council Distinguished Scholar Award for his contributions to the state's culture.